SUPREME DIABETIC COOKBOOK FOR BEGINNERS

Essential Recipes for Balanced Blood Sugar and Healthy Living

MADIE MERTZ

Copyright © 2024 by MADIE MERTZ. All rights reserved. No part of this publication may be reproduced, distributed, or transmitted in any form or by any means, including photocopying, recording, or other electronic or mechanical methods, without the prior written permission of the publisher, except in the case of brief quotations embodied in critical reviews and certain other noncommercial uses permitted by copyright law.

ABOUT THE AUTHOR

Madie Mertz is a culinary expert and a passionate advocate for healthy living. With a background in nutritional science and a love for cooking, Madie has dedicated her career to creating delicious and health-conscious recipes that make managing diabetes both enjoyable and attainable. Her journey into diabetic cooking began when a close family member was diagnosed with diabetes, inspiring her to transform traditional recipes into nutritious, diabetic-friendly meals.

Madie's expertise lies in her ability to blend science and culinary art, crafting dishes that are not only safe for diabetics but also flavorful and satisfying. Her mission is to show that a diabetic diet doesn't have to be bland or restrictive; instead, it can be vibrant, diverse, and full of life.

In "Supreme Diabetic Cookbook for Beginners," Madie shares her wealth of knowledge and practical tips to help readers navigate their dietary needs with confidence and creativity. Each recipe is carefully designed to balance taste and nutrition, making it easier for beginners to embark on their journey toward better health.

Madie lives with her family in a cozy suburban home, where she enjoys experimenting with new recipes, gardening, and spending time outdoors. Her warm, approachable style and dedication to wellness make her a trusted guide in the world of diabetic cooking.

Table of Contents

ABOUT THE AUTHOR 4
Introduction 11
Chapter 1 15
   Breakfast 15
   RECIPES 15
      1. Berry Oatmeal 15
      2. Veggie Scramble 16
      3. Greek Yogurt Parfait 17
      4. Whole Grain Toast with Avocado 18
      5. Spinach and Feta Omelette 19
      6. Smoothie Bowls 20
Chapter 2 21
   Lunch 21
   Nutritional Guidelines for Lunch 21
   RECIPES 22
      1. Quinoa and Black Bean Salad 22
      2. Grilled Chicken and Avocado Wrap 23
      3. Lentil and Vegetable Soup 24

4. Turkey and Veggie Stir-Fry 25

5. Mediterranean Chickpea Salad 26

6. Spinach and Feta Stuffed Peppers 27

Chapter 3 29

Dinner 29

RECIPES 29

1. Baked Salmon with Asparagus 29

2. Stuffed Bell Peppers 30

3. Chicken and Broccoli Stir-Fry 31

4. Beef and Vegetable Stew 32

5. Shrimp and Zucchini Noodles 34

6. Tofu and Veggie Skewers 35

Chapter 4 37

Snacks and Appetizers 37

RECIPES 37

1. Hummus with Veggie Sticks 37

2. Greek Yogurt Dip with Cucumbers 38

3. Almond and Cranberry Trail Mix 39

4. Spicy Roasted Chickpeas 39

5. Cheese and Apple Slices 40

6. Avocado Deviled Eggs 41

Chapter 5 43

Desserts 43
   RECIPES 43
      1. Chocolate Chia Pudding 43
      2. Baked Apples with Cinnamon 44
      3. Almond Flour Cookies 45
      4. Berry Sorbet 46
      5. Peanut Butter Energy Balls 47
      6. Lemon Yogurt Parfait 48

Chapter 6 49
   Drinks 49
   RECIPES 49
      1. Green Smoothie 49
      2. Iced Herbal Tea 50
      3. Lemon Water Infusion 51
      4. Berry Protein Shake 51
      5. Coconut Water with Lime 52
      6. Almond Milk Latte 53

Chapter 7 55
   Special Occasions 55
   RECIPES 55
      1. Herb-Roasted Turkey 55
      2. Stuffed Bell Peppers 56

3. Grilled Salmon with Mango Salsa 57

  4. Baked Chicken Parmesan 58

  5. Holiday Stuffing with Nuts 59

  6. Low-Sugar Pumpkin Pie 61

Chapter 8 63

  Meal Planning and Prep 63

    Benefits of Meal Planning 63

    Tips for Efficient Meal Prep 64

    Weekly Meal Plan Example 64

    Shopping List Guide 65

  Recipes 65

    1. Baked Salmon with Asparagus 65

    2. Quinoa Salad with Lemon Vinaigrette 66

    3. Chicken and Broccoli Casserole 67

    4. Shrimp and Zucchini Noodles 68

    5. Turkey and Hummus Sandwich 69

    6. Beef and Vegetable Stew 70

Chapter 9 73

  Snacks and Appetizers 73

    Importance of Healthy Snacks 73

    Tips for Smart Snacking 74

  Recipes 74

1. Hummus with Veggie Sticks 74

2. Greek Yogurt Dip with Cucumbers 75

3. Almond and Cranberry Trail Mix 76

4. Spicy Roasted Chickpeas 76

5. Cheese and Apple Slices 77

6. Avocado Deviled Eggs 78

Chapter 10 79

Desserts 79

Enjoying Desserts Responsibly 79

Recipes 80

1. Chocolate Chia Pudding 80

2. Baked Apples with Cinnamon 80

3. Almond Flour Cookies 81

4. Berry Sorbet 82

5. Peanut Butter Energy Balls 83

6. Lemon Yogurt Parfait 83

Conclusion 85

Embracing a Healthy Lifestyle 85

Staying Motivated 86

INTRODUCTION

Welcome to the "Supreme Diabetic Cookbook for Beginners." If you've recently been diagnosed with diabetes or are simply looking to better manage your blood sugar levels through diet, you've come to the right place. This cookbook is designed to provide you with a wealth of delicious, easy-to-make recipes that are not only diabetic-friendly but also flavorful and satisfying.

Understanding Diabetes and Diet

Diabetes is a chronic condition that affects millions of people worldwide. It occurs when the body either cannot produce enough insulin or cannot effectively use the insulin it produces. This leads to elevated blood sugar levels, which can have serious health implications if not properly managed.

Diet plays a crucial role in managing diabetes. By choosing the right foods, you can help maintain stable blood sugar levels, prevent complications, and improve your overall health. This cookbook focuses on nutrient-dense ingredients, balanced meals, and portion control to support a healthy lifestyle.

Benefits of a Diabetic-Friendly Diet

Adopting a diabetic-friendly diet offers numerous benefits, including:

- **Improved Blood Sugar Control:** Balanced meals with the right mix of carbohydrates, proteins, and fats can help regulate your blood sugar levels.
- **Enhanced Energy Levels:** Eating nutrient-rich foods can boost your energy and keep you feeling full and satisfied throughout the day.
- **Weight Management:** Many diabetic-friendly recipes are low in calories and high in fiber, which can aid in weight loss and maintenance.
- **Reduced Risk of Complications:** Proper diet management can lower the risk of diabetes-related complications, such as heart disease, kidney damage, and neuropathy.

Essential Ingredients and Tools

Before you dive into the recipes, it's important to familiarize yourself with some key ingredients and tools that will make your cooking experience enjoyable and efficient.

- **Whole Grains:** Opt for whole grains like quinoa, brown rice, and whole-wheat bread, which have a lower glycemic index and provide sustained energy.
- **Lean Proteins:** Incorporate lean proteins such as chicken, turkey, fish, tofu, and legumes into your meals to support muscle health and satiety.
- **Healthy Fats:** Use healthy fats from sources like olive oil, avocados, nuts, and seeds to promote heart health and add flavor to your dishes.

- **Fresh Vegetables and Fruits:** Fill your plate with a variety of colorful vegetables and low-sugar fruits to ensure you get a wide range of vitamins and minerals.
- **Herbs and Spices:** Enhance the flavor of your meals without adding extra sugar or salt by using herbs and spices like basil, cinnamon, turmeric, and garlic.

In addition to these ingredients, having the right tools in your kitchen can make meal preparation more efficient. Some essential tools include a good set of knives, cutting boards, measuring cups and spoons, a blender, and non-stick cookware.

Embarking on Your Culinary Journey

This cookbook is divided into several chapters, each focusing on a different meal of the day or occasion. From hearty breakfasts to satisfying lunches, nourishing dinners, and even indulgent desserts, you'll find a variety of recipes that cater to your tastes and dietary needs.

Each recipe is accompanied by nutritional information, preparation tips, and serving suggestions to help you make informed choices. Whether you're a novice cook or an experienced chef, the "Supreme Diabetic Cookbook for Beginners" is here to guide you on your culinary journey towards better health.

So, grab your apron, stock up on fresh ingredients, and let's get cooking! Your journey to delicious, diabetic-friendly meals starts now.

CHAPTER 1

BREAKFAST

A nutritious breakfast is essential for maintaining stable blood sugar levels and providing energy to start your day. In this chapter, you'll find a variety of diabetic-friendly breakfast recipes that are delicious, easy to prepare, and packed with nutrients.

RECIPES

1. BERRY OATMEAL

Ingredients:

- 1 cup rolled oats
- 2 cups water or unsweetened almond milk
- 1 cup mixed berries (blueberries, strawberries, raspberries)
- 1 tablespoon chia seeds

- 1 teaspoon cinnamon
- 1 teaspoon vanilla extract
- 1 tablespoon chopped nuts (optional)

Prep Time: 5 minutes
Cooking Time: 10 minutes
Servings: 2

Instructions:

1. In a medium saucepan, bring the water or almond milk to a boil.
2. Add the rolled oats, reduce heat, and simmer for about 5 minutes, stirring occasionally.
3. Stir in the berries, chia seeds, cinnamon, and vanilla extract. Cook for another 2-3 minutes until the oats are fully cooked and creamy.
4. Serve topped with chopped nuts if desired.

2. VEGGIE SCRAMBLE

Ingredients:

- 4 large eggs or egg whites
- 1 tablespoon olive oil
- 1 small onion, diced
- 1 bell pepper, diced
- 1 cup spinach, chopped
- 1/2 cup cherry tomatoes, halved
- Salt and pepper to taste

Prep Time: 5 minutes
Cooking Time: 10 minutes
Servings: 2

Instructions:

1. Heat the olive oil in a non-stick skillet over medium heat.
2. Add the onion and bell pepper, sautéing until softened, about 3-4 minutes.
3. Stir in the spinach and cherry tomatoes, cooking until the spinach is wilted.
4. Whisk the eggs in a bowl, then pour into the skillet. Cook, stirring occasionally, until the eggs are scrambled and fully cooked. Season with salt and pepper to taste.

3. GREEK YOGURT PARFAIT

Ingredients:

- 2 cups plain Greek yogurt
- 1 cup mixed berries (strawberries, blueberries, raspberries)
- 1/4 cup granola (low-sugar)
- 1 tablespoon chia seeds
- 1 tablespoon honey or sugar substitute

Prep Time: 5 minutes
Cooking Time: 0 minutes
Servings: 2

Instructions:

1. In two serving glasses or bowls, layer half of the Greek yogurt.
2. Add a layer of mixed berries, followed by a sprinkle of granola and chia seeds.
3. Repeat the layers with the remaining ingredients.
4. Drizzle with honey or your preferred sugar substitute before serving.

4. WHOLE GRAIN TOAST WITH AVOCADO

Ingredients:

- 4 slices whole grain bread
- 2 ripe avocados
- 1 tablespoon lemon juice
- Salt and pepper to taste
- Optional toppings: cherry tomatoes, red pepper flakes, fresh herbs

Prep Time: 5 minutes
Cooking Time: 5 minutes
Servings: 2

Instructions:

1. Toast the whole grain bread slices until golden and crisp.
2. In a bowl, mash the avocados with lemon juice, salt, and pepper.
3. Spread the mashed avocado evenly over the toasted bread.
4. Add any optional toppings as desired before serving.

5. SPINACH AND FETA OMELETTE

Ingredients:

- 4 large eggs
- 1 tablespoon olive oil
- 1/2 cup spinach, chopped
- 1/4 cup feta cheese, crumbled
- Salt and pepper to taste

Prep Time: 5 minutes
Cooking Time: 10 minutes
Servings: 2

Instructions:

1. In a bowl, whisk the eggs with a pinch of salt and pepper.
2. Heat the olive oil in a non-stick skillet over medium heat.
3. Pour the eggs into the skillet, cooking until they begin to set around the edges.

4. Sprinkle the spinach and feta cheese over half of the omelette.
5. Fold the omelette in half, continuing to cook until the eggs are fully set.
6. Serve hot, cut into portions.

6. SMOOTHIE BOWLS

Ingredients:

- 2 cups unsweetened almond milk
- 2 cups frozen mixed berries
- 1 banana
- 2 tablespoons chia seeds
- 1/4 cup granola (low-sugar)
- Fresh berries and mint for garnish

Prep Time: 5 minutes
Cooking Time: 0 minutes
Servings: 2

Instructions:

1. In a blender, combine the almond milk, frozen berries, banana, and chia seeds. Blend until smooth and thick.
2. Pour the smoothie mixture into two bowls.
3. Top each bowl with granola, fresh berries, and mint.
4. Serve immediately.

CHAPTER 2

LUNCH

Nutritional Guidelines for Lunch

A balanced lunch can provide the energy you need to get through the rest of your day. Aim for a mix of lean protein, healthy fats, whole grains, and plenty of vegetables to keep your blood sugar levels stable.

RECIPES

1. QUINOA AND BLACK BEAN SALAD

Ingredients:

- 1 cup quinoa
- 2 cups water
- 1 can (15 oz) black beans, rinsed and drained
- 1 red bell pepper, diced
- 1 small red onion, finely chopped
- 1 cup corn kernels (fresh, frozen, or canned)
- 1/4 cup fresh cilantro, chopped
- Juice of 2 limes
- 2 tablespoons olive oil
- 1 teaspoon cumin
- Salt and pepper to taste

Prep Time: 10 minutes
Cooking Time: 20 minutes
Servings: 4

Instructions:

1. Rinse quinoa under cold water. In a medium saucepan, combine quinoa and water. Bring to a

boil, reduce heat, cover, and simmer for 15-20 minutes, or until water is absorbed.
2. In a large bowl, combine cooked quinoa, black beans, bell pepper, onion, corn, and cilantro.
3. In a small bowl, whisk together lime juice, olive oil, cumin, salt, and pepper.
4. Pour the dressing over the salad and toss to combine.
5. Serve immediately or refrigerate for later.

2. GRILLED CHICKEN AND AVOCADO WRAP

Ingredients:

- 2 boneless, skinless chicken breasts
- 1 tablespoon olive oil
- 1 teaspoon paprika
- Salt and pepper to taste
- 4 whole-wheat tortillas
- 1 avocado, sliced
- 1 cup baby spinach leaves
- 1/2 cup Greek yogurt
- 1 tablespoon lemon juice

Prep Time: 15 minutes
Cooking Time: 15 minutes
Servings: 4

Instructions:

1. Preheat the grill to medium-high heat.
2. Brush chicken breasts with olive oil and season with paprika, salt, and pepper.
3. Grill chicken for 6-7 minutes per side, or until fully cooked. Let cool slightly, then slice thinly.
4. In a small bowl, mix Greek yogurt and lemon juice.
5. Lay out tortillas and spread each with a layer of the yogurt mixture.
6. Top with sliced chicken, avocado, and spinach.
7. Roll up the tortillas and serve immediately.

3. LENTIL AND VEGETABLE SOUP

Ingredients:

- 1 cup green lentils, rinsed
- 1 tablespoon olive oil
- 1 onion, chopped
- 2 carrots, chopped
- 2 celery stalks, chopped
- 3 garlic cloves, minced
- 1 can (14.5 oz) diced tomatoes
- 4 cups low-sodium vegetable broth
- 1 teaspoon dried thyme
- 1 bay leaf
- Salt and pepper to taste
- 2 cups fresh spinach leaves

Prep Time: 10 minutes
Cooking Time: 40 minutes
Servings: 4

Instructions:

1. In a large pot, heat olive oil over medium heat. Add onion, carrots, and celery. Cook until vegetables are softened, about 5 minutes.
2. Add garlic and cook for another minute.
3. Stir in lentils, diced tomatoes, vegetable broth, thyme, bay leaf, salt, and pepper.
4. Bring to a boil, then reduce heat and simmer for 30 minutes, or until lentils are tender.
5. Stir in spinach and cook until wilted, about 2 minutes.
6. Remove bay leaf and serve hot.

4. TURKEY AND VEGGIE STIR-FRY

Ingredients:

- 1 tablespoon olive oil
- 1 lb ground turkey
- 1 red bell pepper, sliced
- 1 yellow bell pepper, sliced
- 1 zucchini, sliced
- 2 cups broccoli florets
- 3 garlic cloves, minced
- 1/4 cup low-sodium soy sauce
- 1 tablespoon rice vinegar

- 1 teaspoon sesame oil
- 1 teaspoon ginger, grated
- 2 green onions, sliced

Prep Time: 10 minutes
Cooking Time: 15 minutes
Servings: 4

Instructions:

1. Heat olive oil in a large skillet over medium-high heat. Add ground turkey and cook until browned, breaking it up with a spoon, about 5 minutes.
2. Add bell peppers, zucchini, broccoli, and garlic. Cook until vegetables are tender, about 7 minutes.
3. In a small bowl, whisk together soy sauce, rice vinegar, sesame oil, and ginger.
4. Pour sauce over the stir-fry and toss to coat.
5. Garnish with green onions and serve immediately.

5. MEDITERRANEAN CHICKPEA SALAD

Ingredients:

- 1 can (15 oz) chickpeas, rinsed and drained
- 1 cucumber, diced
- 1 cup cherry tomatoes, halved
- 1/4 cup red onion, finely chopped
- 1/4 cup Kalamata olives, sliced

- 1/4 cup feta cheese, crumbled
- 2 tablespoons olive oil
- 1 tablespoon red wine vinegar
- 1 teaspoon dried oregano
- Salt and pepper to taste

Prep Time: 10 minutes
Cooking Time: 0 minutes
Servings: 4

Instructions:

1. In a large bowl, combine chickpeas, cucumber, cherry tomatoes, red onion, olives, and feta cheese.
2. In a small bowl, whisk together olive oil, red wine vinegar, oregano, salt, and pepper.
3. Pour dressing over the salad and toss to combine.
4. Serve immediately or refrigerate for later.

6. SPINACH AND FETA STUFFED PEPPERS

Ingredients:

- 4 large bell peppers
- 1 tablespoon olive oil
- 1 onion, chopped
- 2 garlic cloves, minced

- 1 cup cooked quinoa
- 2 cups fresh spinach, chopped
- 1/2 cup feta cheese, crumbled
- 1 teaspoon dried oregano
- Salt and pepper to taste

Prep Time: 15 minutes
Cooking Time: 30 minutes
Servings: 4

Instructions:

1. Preheat oven to 375°F (190°C). Cut tops off bell peppers and remove seeds.
2. In a large skillet, heat olive oil over medium heat. Add onion and cook until softened, about 5 minutes.
3. Add garlic and cook for another minute.
4. Stir in quinoa, spinach, feta cheese, oregano, salt, and pepper. Cook until spinach is wilted, about 2 minutes.
5. Stuff bell peppers with the quinoa mixture and place in a baking dish.
6. Bake for 25-30 minutes, or until peppers are tender.
7. Serve hot.

CHAPTER 3

DINNER

Dinner is an essential meal that helps to wind down the day while providing the necessary nutrients to keep your blood sugar levels stable overnight. The following recipes are designed to be balanced, delicious, and supportive of your diabetic diet.

RECIPES

1. BAKED SALMON WITH ASPARAGUS

Ingredients:

- 4 salmon fillets (about 4 oz each)
- 1 bunch asparagus, trimmed
- 2 tbsp olive oil
- 2 cloves garlic, minced
- 1 lemon, sliced
- Salt and pepper to taste
- 1 tsp dried dill

Prep Time: 10 minutes
Cooking Time: 20 minutes
Servings: 4

Instructions:

1. Preheat your oven to 400°F (200°C).
2. Arrange the salmon fillets and asparagus on a baking sheet.
3. Drizzle with olive oil and sprinkle with garlic, salt, pepper, and dill.
4. Top with lemon slices.
5. Bake for 20 minutes, or until the salmon is cooked through and the asparagus is tender.
6. Serve immediately.

2. STUFFED BELL PEPPERS

Ingredients:

- 4 large bell peppers, tops cut off and seeds removed
- 1 lb lean ground turkey
- 1 cup cooked quinoa
- 1 small onion, diced
- 2 cloves garlic, minced
- 1 cup diced tomatoes
- 1 tsp dried oregano
- 1 tsp dried basil
- Salt and pepper to taste
- 1/2 cup shredded mozzarella cheese

Prep Time: 15 minutes
Cooking Time: 45 minutes
Servings: 4

Instructions:

1. Preheat your oven to 375°F (190°C).
2. In a large skillet, cook the ground turkey over medium heat until browned. Drain any excess fat.
3. Add the onion and garlic to the skillet and sauté until softened.
4. Stir in the cooked quinoa, diced tomatoes, oregano, basil, salt, and pepper.
5. Stuff each bell pepper with the turkey mixture and place them in a baking dish.
6. Cover with foil and bake for 35 minutes.
7. Remove the foil, sprinkle the tops with cheese, and bake for an additional 10 minutes, or until the cheese is melted and bubbly.
8. Serve hot.

3. CHICKEN AND BROCCOLI STIR-FRY

Ingredients:

- 1 lb boneless, skinless chicken breasts, cut into strips
- 2 cups broccoli florets
- 1 red bell pepper, sliced
- 2 cloves garlic, minced
- 1 tbsp ginger, grated

- 3 tbsp soy sauce (low sodium)
- 1 tbsp sesame oil
- 1 tbsp olive oil
- 1 tbsp cornstarch
- 1/4 cup water
- 2 green onions, sliced

Prep Time: 15 minutes
Cooking Time: 15 minutes
Servings: 4

Instructions:

1. In a small bowl, mix the cornstarch and water to make a slurry.
2. Heat the olive oil in a large skillet or wok over medium-high heat.
3. Add the chicken strips and cook until browned and cooked through. Remove from the skillet and set aside.
4. In the same skillet, add the sesame oil, garlic, and ginger, and sauté for 1 minute.
5. Add the broccoli and red bell pepper, and stir-fry for 3-4 minutes until tender-crisp.
6. Return the chicken to the skillet, add the soy sauce and cornstarch slurry, and cook for another 2-3 minutes until the sauce thickens.
7. Garnish with green onions and serve immediately.

4. BEEF AND VEGETABLE STEW

Ingredients:

- 1 lb lean beef stew meat, cut into cubes
- 2 tbsp olive oil
- 1 onion, chopped
- 2 cloves garlic, minced
- 3 carrots, sliced
- 2 celery stalks, sliced
- 3 cups low-sodium beef broth
- 1 cup water
- 1 cup diced tomatoes
- 2 potatoes, diced
- 1 tsp dried thyme
- 1 bay leaf
- Salt and pepper to taste

Prep Time: 15 minutes
Cooking Time: 2 hours
Servings: 6

Instructions:

1. In a large pot, heat the olive oil over medium-high heat.
2. Add the beef cubes and brown on all sides. Remove the beef and set aside.
3. Add the onion and garlic to the pot and sauté until softened.

4. Return the beef to the pot and add the carrots, celery, beef broth, water, tomatoes, potatoes, thyme, bay leaf, salt, and pepper.
5. Bring to a boil, then reduce the heat to low and simmer for 2 hours, or until the beef is tender and the vegetables are cooked through.
6. Remove the bay leaf before serving.

5. SHRIMP AND ZUCCHINI NOODLES

Ingredients:

- 1 lb large shrimp, peeled and deveined
- 2 large zucchinis, spiralized into noodles
- 2 tbsp olive oil
- 3 cloves garlic, minced
- 1/4 tsp red pepper flakes
- 1 lemon, juiced
- Salt and pepper to taste
- 1/4 cup grated Parmesan cheese
- Fresh parsley, chopped (for garnish)

Prep Time: 10 minutes
Cooking Time: 10 minutes
Servings: 4

Instructions:

1. Heat the olive oil in a large skillet over medium heat.

2. Add the garlic and red pepper flakes, and sauté for 1 minute.
3. Add the shrimp and cook until pink and opaque, about 3-4 minutes.
4. Remove the shrimp from the skillet and set aside.
5. Add the zucchini noodles to the skillet and cook for 2-3 minutes until tender.
6. Return the shrimp to the skillet, add the lemon juice, salt, and pepper, and toss to combine.
7. Sprinkle with Parmesan cheese and garnish with fresh parsley before serving.

6. TOFU AND VEGGIE SKEWERS

Ingredients:

- 1 block firm tofu, drained and cubed
- 1 red bell pepper, cut into chunks
- 1 yellow bell pepper, cut into chunks
- 1 zucchini, sliced
- 1 red onion, cut into chunks
- 2 tbsp olive oil
- 2 tbsp soy sauce (low sodium)
- 1 tbsp balsamic vinegar
- 1 tsp dried oregano
- Salt and pepper to taste
- Wooden skewers, soaked in water for 30 minutes

Prep Time: 15 minutes
Cooking Time: 15 minutes
Servings: 4

Instructions:

1. Preheat your grill or grill pan over medium-high heat.
2. In a bowl, mix the olive oil, soy sauce, balsamic vinegar, oregano, salt, and pepper.
3. Thread the tofu, bell peppers, zucchini, and red onion onto the skewers.
4. Brush the skewers with the marinade and place them on the grill.
5. Grill for 10-15 minutes, turning occasionally, until the vegetables are tender and the tofu is slightly charred.
6. Serve hot.

CHAPTER 4

SNACKS AND APPETIZERS

RECIPES

1. HUMMUS WITH VEGGIE STICKS

Ingredients:

- 1 can (15 oz) chickpeas, drained and rinsed
- 1/4 cup tahini
- 2 tbsp olive oil
- 2 cloves garlic, minced
- 1 lemon, juiced
- 1/2 tsp ground cumin
- Salt to taste
- Assorted veggie sticks (carrots, celery, bell peppers, cucumbers)

Prep Time: 10 minutes
Cooking Time: None
Servings: 4

Instructions:

1. In a food processor, combine chickpeas, tahini, olive oil, garlic, lemon juice, cumin, and salt.
2. Blend until smooth, adding water if necessary to reach desired consistency.
3. Serve with assorted veggie sticks.

2. GREEK YOGURT DIP WITH CUCUMBERS

Ingredients:

- 1 cup plain Greek yogurt
- 1 clove garlic, minced
- 1 tbsp fresh dill, chopped
- 1 tbsp lemon juice
- Salt and pepper to taste
- 2 cucumbers, sliced

Prep Time: 10 minutes
Cooking Time: None
Servings: 4

Instructions:

1. In a bowl, combine Greek yogurt, garlic, dill, lemon juice, salt, and pepper.
2. Mix well until all ingredients are incorporated.
3. Serve with sliced cucumbers.

3. ALMOND AND CRANBERRY TRAIL MIX

Ingredients:

- 1 cup raw almonds
- 1/2 cup unsweetened dried cranberries
- 1/4 cup pumpkin seeds
- 1/4 cup sunflower seeds

Prep Time: 5 minutes
Cooking Time: None
Servings: 4

Instructions:

1. In a large bowl, combine almonds, dried cranberries, pumpkin seeds, and sunflower seeds.
2. Mix well and divide into portions.

4. SPICY ROASTED CHICKPEAS

Ingredients:

- 1 can (15 oz) chickpeas, drained and rinsed
- 1 tbsp olive oil

- 1 tsp paprika
- 1/2 tsp cayenne pepper
- 1/2 tsp garlic powder
- Salt to taste

Prep Time: 10 minutes
Cooking Time: 30 minutes
Servings: 4

Instructions:

1. Preheat oven to 400°F (200°C).
2. In a bowl, toss chickpeas with olive oil, paprika, cayenne pepper, garlic powder, and salt.
3. Spread chickpeas on a baking sheet in a single layer.
4. Roast for 30 minutes, stirring halfway through, until crispy.
5. Let cool and serve.

5. CHEESE AND APPLE SLICES

Ingredients:

- 1 large apple, sliced
- 4 oz cheddar cheese, sliced

Prep Time: 5 minutes
Cooking Time: None
Servings: 4

Instructions:

1. Arrange apple slices and cheddar cheese slices on a platter.
2. Serve immediately.

6. AVOCADO DEVILED EGGS

Ingredients:

- 6 large eggs, hard-boiled and peeled
- 1 avocado, peeled and pitted
- 1 tbsp lime juice
- 1 tbsp Greek yogurt
- 1 clove garlic, minced
- Salt and pepper to taste
- Paprika for garnish

Prep Time: 15 minutes
Cooking Time: None
Servings: 6

Instructions:

1. Cut eggs in half lengthwise and remove yolks.
2. In a bowl, mash avocado with lime juice, Greek yogurt, garlic, salt, and pepper.
3. Spoon avocado mixture into egg whites.
4. Sprinkle with paprika for garnish.
5. Serve chilled.

CHAPTER 5

DESSERTS

Desserts are often seen as a challenge for those managing diabetes, but it's entirely possible to enjoy sweet treats without compromising your health. This chapter offers a selection of delicious, diabetic-friendly dessert recipes that are low in sugar and high in flavor. Whether you crave chocolate, fruit, or creamy delights, there's something here for every sweet tooth.

RECIPES

1. CHOCOLATE CHIA PUDDING

Ingredients:

- 1/4 cup chia seeds
- 1 cup unsweetened almond milk
- 2 tbsp cocoa powder
- 1-2 tbsp erythritol or preferred sweetener
- 1 tsp vanilla extract

- Fresh berries (optional, for garnish)

Prep Time: 5 minutes
Cooking Time: 0 minutes (4 hours or overnight for chilling)
Servings: 2

Instructions:

1. In a medium bowl, whisk together the almond milk, cocoa powder, erythritol, and vanilla extract until well combined.
2. Add the chia seeds and stir well.
3. Cover and refrigerate for at least 4 hours or overnight, until the mixture thickens to a pudding-like consistency.
4. Serve chilled, topped with fresh berries if desired.

2. BAKED APPLES WITH CINNAMON

Ingredients:

- 4 medium apples, cored
- 1/4 cup chopped nuts (walnuts or pecans)
- 1 tsp ground cinnamon
- 1 tbsp melted coconut oil
- 1-2 tbsp sugar-free maple syrup

Prep Time: 10 minutes
Cooking Time: 25 minutes
Servings: 4

Instructions:

1. Preheat your oven to 375°F (190°C).
2. Place the cored apples in a baking dish.
3. In a small bowl, mix the chopped nuts, cinnamon, coconut oil, and sugar-free maple syrup.
4. Fill the center of each apple with the nut mixture.
5. Bake for 25 minutes or until the apples are tender.
6. Serve warm.

3. ALMOND FLOUR COOKIES

Ingredients:

- 2 cups almond flour
- 1/4 cup erythritol or preferred sweetener
- 1/4 tsp salt
- 1/4 tsp baking soda
- 1/4 cup melted coconut oil
- 1 large egg
- 1 tsp vanilla extract

Prep Time: 10 minutes
Cooking Time: 12 minutes
Servings: 12 cookies

Instructions:

1. Preheat your oven to 350°F (175°C) and line a baking sheet with parchment paper.
2. In a large bowl, whisk together the almond flour, erythritol, salt, and baking soda.
3. Add the melted coconut oil, egg, and vanilla extract to the dry ingredients and mix until a dough forms.
4. Scoop tablespoon-sized balls of dough onto the prepared baking sheet and flatten them slightly.
5. Bake for 10-12 minutes, or until the edges are golden brown.
6. Allow the cookies to cool on the baking sheet before transferring them to a wire rack.

4. BERRY SORBET

Ingredients:

- 2 cups mixed berries (strawberries, blueberries, raspberries)
- 1/4 cup water
- 1-2 tbsp erythritol or preferred sweetener
- 1 tbsp lemon juice

Prep Time: 10 minutes
Cooking Time: 0 minutes (2 hours for freezing)
Servings: 4

Instructions:

1. In a blender, combine the mixed berries, water, erythritol, and lemon juice. Blend until smooth.
2. Pour the mixture into a shallow dish and freeze for about 2 hours, stirring every 30 minutes until the sorbet is firm.
3. Scoop into bowls and serve.

5. PEANUT BUTTER ENERGY BALLS

Ingredients:

- 1 cup rolled oats
- 1/2 cup natural peanut butter
- 1/4 cup flaxseed meal
- 1/4 cup sugar-free chocolate chips
- 1/4 cup honey or sugar-free syrup
- 1 tsp vanilla extract

Prep Time: 10 minutes
Cooking Time: 0 minutes
Servings: 12 balls

Instructions:

1. In a large bowl, combine all the ingredients and mix until well combined.
2. Roll the mixture into 1-inch balls and place them on a baking sheet lined with parchment paper.
3. Refrigerate for about 30 minutes until firm.
4. Store in an airtight container in the refrigerator.

6. LEMON YOGURT PARFAIT

Ingredients:

- 2 cups Greek yogurt
- 1 tbsp lemon zest
- 1 tbsp lemon juice
- 1-2 tbsp erythritol or preferred sweetener
- 1/2 cup fresh berries
- 1/4 cup chopped nuts

Prep Time: 10 minutes
Cooking Time: 0 minutes
Servings: 4

Instructions:

1. In a medium bowl, mix the Greek yogurt, lemon zest, lemon juice, and erythritol until well combined.
2. In serving glasses or bowls, layer the lemon yogurt with fresh berries and chopped nuts.
3. Serve immediately or refrigerate until ready to enjoy.

CHAPTER 6

DRINKS

When managing diabetes, it's important to choose drinks that won't spike your blood sugar levels. This chapter provides a selection of refreshing, flavorful, and diabetic-friendly beverages that are easy to prepare and enjoy at any time of the day.

RECIPES

1. GREEN SMOOTHIE

Ingredients:

- 1 cup unsweetened almond milk
- 1 cup fresh spinach
- 1/2 cup cucumber, peeled and sliced
- 1/2 green apple, cored and chopped
- 1/2 avocado

- 1 tablespoon chia seeds
- Ice cubes (optional)

Prep Time: 10 minutes
Servings: 2

Instructions:

1. Combine all ingredients in a blender.
2. Blend until smooth and creamy.
3. Pour into glasses and serve immediately.

2. ICED HERBAL TEA

Ingredients:

- 4 cups water
- 4 herbal tea bags (e.g., peppermint, chamomile)
- 1 lemon, sliced
- Fresh mint leaves (optional)
- Ice cubes

Prep Time: 5 minutes
Cooking Time: 10 minutes
Servings: 4

Instructions:

1. Bring water to a boil in a saucepan.
2. Remove from heat, add tea bags, and let steep for 5-7 minutes.

3. Remove the tea bags and let the tea cool to room temperature.
4. Pour the tea into a pitcher, and add lemon slices and mint leaves if using.
5. Refrigerate until chilled.
6. Serve over ice.

3. LEMON WATER INFUSION

Ingredients:

- 1 lemon, thinly sliced
- 1 lime, thinly sliced
- 1 small cucumber, thinly sliced
- 8 cups water
- Fresh mint leaves (optional)

Prep Time: 5 minutes
Servings: 8

Instructions:

1. Combine lemon, lime, cucumber slices, and mint leaves in a large pitcher.
2. Fill with water and stir to combine.
3. Refrigerate for at least 2 hours to allow flavors to infuse.
4. Serve chilled.

4. BERRY PROTEIN SHAKE

Ingredients:

- 1 cup unsweetened almond milk
- 1/2 cup mixed berries (strawberries, blueberries, raspberries)
- 1 scoop vanilla protein powder
- 1 tablespoon flaxseeds
- Ice cubes

Prep Time: 5 minutes
Servings: 1

Instructions:

1. Combine all ingredients in a blender.
2. Blend until smooth.
3. Pour into a glass and enjoy immediately.

5. COCONUT WATER WITH LIME

Ingredients:

- 2 cups coconut water
- Juice of 1 lime
- Lime slices for garnish
- Ice cubes

Prep Time: 5 minutes
Servings: 2

Instructions:

1. In a pitcher, combine coconut water and lime juice.
2. Stir well.
3. Pour into glasses over ice.
4. Garnish with lime slices.

6. ALMOND MILK LATTE

Ingredients:

- 1 cup unsweetened almond milk
- 1 shot espresso or 1/2 cup strong brewed coffee
- 1 teaspoon vanilla extract
- 1/2 teaspoon ground cinnamon
- Stevia or your preferred sweetener (optional)

Prep Time: 5 minutes
Cooking Time: 5 minutes
Servings: 1

Instructions:

1. Heat almond milk in a saucepan over medium heat until warm.
2. Stir in vanilla extract and sweetener if using.
3. Brew espresso or coffee.
4. Pour coffee into a mug, then add the warm almond milk mixture.
5. Sprinkle with ground cinnamon.
6. Serve immediately.

CHAPTER 7

SPECIAL OCCASIONS

Special occasions are the perfect time to celebrate with delicious and healthy dishes that everyone will enjoy. Whether it's a holiday gathering, a birthday party, or a family reunion, these recipes are designed to be diabetic-friendly while still feeling indulgent and festive.

RECIPES

1. HERB-ROASTED TURKEY

Ingredients:

- 1 whole turkey (10-12 lbs)
- 1/4 cup olive oil
- 2 tbsp fresh rosemary, chopped
- 2 tbsp fresh thyme, chopped
- 1 tbsp fresh sage, chopped
- 4 cloves garlic, minced
- Salt and pepper to taste

- 1 lemon, halved
- 1 onion, quartered
- 2 cups low-sodium chicken broth

Prep Time: 20 minutes
Cooking Time: 3-4 hours
Servings: 10-12

Instructions:

1. Preheat the oven to 325°F (165°C).
2. In a small bowl, mix olive oil, rosemary, thyme, sage, garlic, salt, and pepper.
3. Rinse the turkey and pat dry. Rub the herb mixture all over the turkey, including under the skin.
4. Place the lemon and onion inside the turkey cavity.
5. Place the turkey on a rack in a roasting pan and pour the chicken broth into the bottom of the pan.
6. Roast the turkey, basting occasionally with the pan juices, until the internal temperature reaches 165°F (74°C) (about 3-4 hours).
7. Let the turkey rest for 20 minutes before carving.

2. STUFFED BELL PEPPERS

Ingredients:

- 4 large bell peppers
- 1 cup quinoa, cooked
- 1 lb lean ground turkey
- 1 onion, diced

- 2 cloves garlic, minced
- 1 cup canned diced tomatoes (no salt added)
- 1 tsp cumin
- 1 tsp paprika
- 1/2 cup shredded low-fat cheddar cheese
- Salt and pepper to taste

Prep Time: 15 minutes
Cooking Time: 40 minutes
Servings: 4

Instructions:

1. Preheat the oven to 375°F (190°C).
2. Cut the tops off the bell peppers and remove the seeds and membranes.
3. In a skillet, cook the ground turkey, onion, and garlic over medium heat until the turkey is browned.
4. Add the cooked quinoa, diced tomatoes, cumin, paprika, salt, and pepper to the skillet. Stir to combine.
5. Stuff the bell peppers with the turkey mixture and place them in a baking dish.
6. Sprinkle the cheese on top of the peppers.
7. Cover with foil and bake for 30 minutes. Remove the foil and bake for an additional 10 minutes until the peppers are tender and the cheese is melted.

3. GRILLED SALMON WITH MANGO SALSA

Ingredients:

- 4 salmon fillets (6 oz each)
- 1 tbsp olive oil
- Salt and pepper to taste
- 1 mango, diced
- 1/2 red onion, diced
- 1/4 cup fresh cilantro, chopped
- 1 jalapeño, seeded and diced
- Juice of 1 lime

Prep Time: 15 minutes
Cooking Time: 15 minutes
Servings: 4

Instructions:

1. Preheat the grill to medium-high heat.
2. Brush the salmon fillets with olive oil and season with salt and pepper.
3. Grill the salmon for 6-8 minutes per side or until the fish flakes easily with a fork.
4. In a bowl, combine the mango, red onion, cilantro, jalapeño, and lime juice.
5. Serve the grilled salmon topped with the mango salsa.

4. BAKED CHICKEN PARMESAN

Ingredients:

- 4 boneless, skinless chicken breasts
- 1/2 cup whole wheat breadcrumbs
- 1/4 cup grated Parmesan cheese
- 1 tsp Italian seasoning
- 1/2 tsp garlic powder
- 1/2 tsp onion powder
- 1 cup marinara sauce (no sugar added)
- 1/2 cup shredded mozzarella cheese
- Salt and pepper to taste

Prep Time: 15 minutes
Cooking Time: 30 minutes
Servings: 4

Instructions:

1. Preheat the oven to 375°F (190°C).
2. In a shallow dish, combine breadcrumbs, Parmesan cheese, Italian seasoning, garlic powder, onion powder, salt, and pepper.
3. Coat the chicken breasts with the breadcrumb mixture.
4. Place the chicken in a baking dish and bake for 20 minutes.
5. Remove from the oven, top with marinara sauce and mozzarella cheese.
6. Return to the oven and bake for an additional 10 minutes until the chicken is cooked through and the cheese is melted and bubbly.

5. HOLIDAY STUFFING WITH NUTS

Ingredients:

- 6 cups whole grain bread cubes
- 1 cup celery, chopped
- 1 cup onion, chopped
- 1/2 cup carrots, chopped
- 1/2 cup walnuts, chopped
- 1/2 cup dried cranberries
- 2 cups low-sodium chicken broth
- 1/4 cup olive oil
- 1 tbsp fresh sage, chopped
- 1 tbsp fresh thyme, chopped
- Salt and pepper to taste

Prep Time: 20 minutes
Cooking Time: 30 minutes
Servings: 6-8

Instructions:

1. Preheat the oven to 350°F (175°C).
2. In a large bowl, combine the bread cubes, celery, onion, carrots, walnuts, and dried cranberries.
3. In a small bowl, whisk together the chicken broth, olive oil, sage, thyme, salt, and pepper.
4. Pour the broth mixture over the bread mixture and toss to combine.
5. Transfer the stuffing to a baking dish and cover with foil.
6. Bake for 20 minutes, then remove the foil and bake for an additional 10 minutes until the top is golden brown.

6. LOW-SUGAR PUMPKIN PIE

Ingredients:

- 1 prepared whole wheat pie crust
- 1 can (15 oz) pumpkin puree
- 1 cup unsweetened almond milk
- 3/4 cup erythritol or other sugar substitute
- 2 eggs
- 1 tsp vanilla extract
- 1 tsp ground cinnamon
- 1/2 tsp ground ginger
- 1/4 tsp ground cloves
- 1/4 tsp ground nutmeg

Prep Time: 15 minutes
Cooking Time: 50 minutes
Servings: 8

Instructions:

1. Preheat the oven to 350°F (175°C).
2. In a large bowl, combine the pumpkin puree, almond milk, erythritol, eggs, vanilla extract, cinnamon, ginger, cloves, and nutmeg.
3. Pour the pumpkin mixture into the pie crust.
4. Bake for 50 minutes, or until a toothpick inserted in the center comes out clean.
5. Allow the pie to cool completely before serving.

CHAPTER 8

MEAL PLANNING AND PREP

BENEFITS OF MEAL PLANNING

Meal planning is a powerful tool in managing diabetes effectively. By planning your meals in advance, you can ensure balanced nutrition, maintain stable blood sugar levels, and avoid the temptation of unhealthy food choices. Here are some key benefits of meal planning:

- **Improved Blood Sugar Control:** Planning meals helps you choose foods that keep your blood sugar levels stable.
- **Time and Money Savings:** Preparing meals ahead of time can save you time and reduce grocery costs by minimizing food waste.
- **Stress Reduction:** Having a plan in place eliminates the daily stress of deciding what to eat, making it easier to stick to a healthy diet.
- **Balanced Nutrition:** Thoughtful planning ensures you get a variety of nutrients necessary for overall health.

TIPS FOR EFFICIENT MEAL PREP

- **Create a Weekly Menu:** Plan your meals for the week, including breakfast, lunch, dinner, and snacks. Consider your schedule and choose recipes that fit your time constraints.
- **Make a Shopping List:** Based on your menu, create a detailed shopping list. Stick to your list to avoid impulse purchases.
- **Prep Ingredients in Advance:** Chop vegetables, marinate proteins, and measure out ingredients ahead of time to streamline the cooking process.
- **Batch Cooking:** Prepare larger portions of meals and store them in the refrigerator or freezer for quick and easy access throughout the week.
- **Use Storage Containers:** Invest in quality storage containers to keep prepped ingredients and cooked meals fresh and organized.

WEEKLY MEAL PLAN EXAMPLE

Here's an example of a weekly meal plan to help you get started:

- **Monday:** Baked Salmon with Asparagus
- **Tuesday:** Quinoa Salad with Lemon Vinaigrette
- **Wednesday:** Chicken and Broccoli Casserole
- **Thursday:** Shrimp and Zucchini Noodles
- **Friday:** Turkey and Hummus Sandwich
- **Saturday:** Beef and Vegetable Stew
- **Sunday:** Tofu and Veggie Skewers

SHOPPING LIST GUIDE

To accompany the weekly meal plan, here's a basic shopping list:

- **Proteins:** Salmon, chicken breast, shrimp, turkey, tofu
- **Grains:** Quinoa, whole-wheat bread
- **Vegetables:** Asparagus, broccoli, zucchini, mixed salad greens, bell peppers, carrots, onions
- **Fruits:** Lemons, berries, apples
- **Pantry Staples:** Olive oil, hummus, spices (garlic, basil, cinnamon, turmeric), low-sodium broth
- **Dairy:** Greek yogurt, feta cheese

RECIPES

1. BAKED SALMON WITH ASPARAGUS

Ingredients:

- 4 salmon fillets
- 1 bunch asparagus, trimmed
- 2 tbsp olive oil

- 1 lemon, sliced
- 2 garlic cloves, minced
- Salt and pepper to taste

Prep Time: 10 minutes
Cooking Time: 20 minutes
Servings: 4

Instructions:

1. Preheat oven to 400°F (200°C).
2. Place salmon fillets and asparagus on a baking sheet.
3. Drizzle with olive oil and sprinkle with minced garlic, salt, and pepper.
4. Arrange lemon slices over salmon and asparagus.
5. Bake for 20 minutes or until salmon is cooked through and asparagus is tender.
6. Serve immediately.

2. QUINOA SALAD WITH LEMON VINAIGRETTE

Ingredients:

- 1 cup quinoa, rinsed
- 2 cups water
- 1 cucumber, diced
- 1 bell pepper, diced
- 1 cup cherry tomatoes, halved
- 1/4 cup red onion, finely chopped

- 1/4 cup fresh parsley, chopped
- 3 tbsp olive oil
- 1 lemon, juiced
- Salt and pepper to taste

Prep Time: 15 minutes
Cooking Time: 15 minutes
Servings: 4

Instructions:

1. In a medium pot, bring quinoa and water to a boil. Reduce heat, cover, and simmer for 15 minutes or until water is absorbed and quinoa is tender.
2. In a large bowl, combine cooked quinoa, cucumber, bell pepper, cherry tomatoes, red onion, and parsley.
3. In a small bowl, whisk together olive oil, lemon juice, salt, and pepper.
4. Pour vinaigrette over the salad and toss to combine.
5. Serve chilled or at room temperature.

3. CHICKEN AND BROCCOLI CASSEROLE

Ingredients:

- 2 cups cooked chicken breast, shredded
- 4 cups broccoli florets
- 1 cup low-fat Greek yogurt

- 1/2 cup low-fat shredded cheddar cheese
- 1/4 cup grated Parmesan cheese
- 1 tsp garlic powder
- Salt and pepper to taste

Prep Time: 15 minutes
Cooking Time: 25 minutes
Servings: 4

Instructions:

1. Preheat oven to 375°F (190°C).
2. Steam broccoli until tender.
3. In a large bowl, combine shredded chicken, steamed broccoli, Greek yogurt, cheddar cheese, Parmesan cheese, garlic powder, salt, and pepper.
4. Transfer mixture to a baking dish.
5. Bake for 25 minutes or until bubbly and golden brown.
6. Serve warm.

4. SHRIMP AND ZUCCHINI NOODLES

Ingredients:

- 1 lb shrimp, peeled and deveined
- 4 medium zucchinis, spiralized
- 2 tbsp olive oil
- 3 garlic cloves, minced
- 1/4 cup fresh parsley, chopped
- Juice of 1 lemon

- Salt and pepper to taste

Prep Time: 15 minutes
Cooking Time: 10 minutes
Servings: 4

Instructions:

1. Heat olive oil in a large skillet over medium heat.
2. Add garlic and sauté for 1 minute.
3. Add shrimp and cook until pink and opaque, about 3-4 minutes.
4. Remove shrimp from skillet and set aside.
5. In the same skillet, add zucchini noodles and cook for 2-3 minutes until tender.
6. Return shrimp to skillet, add lemon juice, parsley, salt, and pepper.
7. Toss to combine and serve immediately.

5. TURKEY AND HUMMUS SANDWICH

Ingredients:

- 4 slices whole-wheat bread
- 8 oz sliced turkey breast
- 1/2 cup hummus
- 1 cup mixed salad greens
- 1 tomato, sliced
- Salt and pepper to taste

Prep Time: 10 minutes
Cooking Time: N/A
Servings: 2

Instructions:

1. Spread hummus on each slice of whole-wheat bread.
2. Layer turkey slices, mixed salad greens, and tomato slices on two of the bread slices.
3. Season with salt and pepper.
4. Top with remaining bread slices.
5. Cut sandwiches in half and serve.

6. BEEF AND VEGETABLE STEW

Ingredients:

- 1 lb beef stew meat, cubed
- 4 cups low-sodium beef broth
- 2 cups carrots, sliced
- 2 cups potatoes, diced
- 1 onion, chopped
- 2 garlic cloves, minced
- 1 cup green beans, trimmed
- 2 tbsp olive oil
- 1 tsp dried thyme
- Salt and pepper to taste

Prep Time: 20 minutes
Cooking Time: 1 hour 30 minutes
Servings: 6

Instructions:

1. Heat olive oil in a large pot over medium heat.
2. Add beef stew meat and brown on all sides.
3. Add chopped onion and garlic, sauté until translucent.
4. Pour in beef broth, add carrots, potatoes, thyme, salt, and pepper.
5. Bring to a boil, then reduce heat and simmer for 1 hour.
6. Add green beans and continue to simmer for an additional 30 minutes until vegetables are tender.
7. Serve hot.

CHAPTER 9

SNACKS AND APPETIZERS

IMPORTANCE OF HEALTHY SNACKS

Snacking can play an important role in managing diabetes by preventing blood sugar spikes and keeping hunger at bay. Choosing healthy, nutrient-dense snacks can help maintain energy levels and provide essential vitamins and minerals. Here are some benefits of incorporating healthy snacks into your diet:

- **Blood Sugar Control:** Eating small, balanced snacks can help keep blood sugar levels stable between meals.
- **Improved Satiety:** Healthy snacks can keep you feeling full and satisfied, reducing the temptation to overeat during meals.
- **Nutritional Boost:** Snacks provide an opportunity to add extra nutrients to your diet, such as fiber, protein, and healthy fats.

TIPS FOR SMART SNACKING

- **Plan Ahead:** Prepare snacks in advance to ensure you have healthy options readily available.
- **Portion Control:** Be mindful of portion sizes to avoid overeating.
- **Balance Nutrients:** Choose snacks that combine protein, healthy fats, and fiber for sustained energy.

RECIPES

1. HUMMUS WITH VEGGIE STICKS

Ingredients:

- 1 can chickpeas, drained and rinsed
- 2 tbsp tahini
- 2 tbsp olive oil
- 2 garlic cloves, minced
- Juice of 1 lemon
- Salt and pepper to taste
- Assorted veggie sticks (carrots, cucumbers, bell peppers)

Prep Time: 10 minutes
Cooking Time: N/A
Servings: 4

Instructions:

1. In a food processor, combine chickpeas, tahini, olive oil, garlic, lemon juice, salt, and pepper.
2. Blend until smooth.
3. Serve with assorted veggie sticks.

2. GREEK YOGURT DIP WITH CUCUMBERS

Ingredients:

- 1 cup plain Greek yogurt
- 1 tbsp fresh dill, chopped
- 1 tbsp lemon juice
- 1 garlic clove, minced
- Salt and pepper to taste
- 2 cucumbers, sliced

Prep Time: 10 minutes
Cooking Time: N/A
Servings: 4

Instructions:

1. In a bowl, combine Greek yogurt, dill, lemon juice, garlic, salt, and pepper.

2. Mix well.
3. Serve with cucumber slices.

3. ALMOND AND CRANBERRY TRAIL MIX

Ingredients:

- 1 cup raw almonds
- 1/2 cup dried cranberries (unsweetened)
- 1/4 cup pumpkin seeds
- 1/4 cup sunflower seeds

Prep Time: 5 minutes
Cooking Time: N/A
Servings: 4

Instructions:

1. In a bowl, combine almonds, cranberries, pumpkin seeds, and sunflower seeds.
2. Mix well.
3. Divide into portions and store in airtight containers.

4. SPICY ROASTED CHICKPEAS

Ingredients:

- 1 can chickpeas, drained and rinsed
- 2 tbsp olive oil

- 1 tsp smoked paprika
- 1/2 tsp cayenne pepper
- 1/2 tsp garlic powder
- Salt to taste

Prep Time: 10 minutes
Cooking Time: 30 minutes
Servings: 4

Instructions:

1. Preheat oven to 400°F (200°C).
2. Pat chickpeas dry with a paper towel.
3. In a bowl, toss chickpeas with olive oil, smoked paprika, cayenne pepper, garlic powder, and salt.
4. Spread chickpeas on a baking sheet.
5. Bake for 30 minutes, shaking the pan halfway through, until crispy.
6. Let cool and serve.

5. CHEESE AND APPLE SLICES

Ingredients:

- 1 apple, sliced
- 2 oz low-fat cheese (such as cheddar or mozzarella), sliced

Prep Time: 5 minutes
Cooking Time: N/A
Servings: 2

Instructions:

1. Arrange apple and cheese slices on a plate.
2. Serve immediately.

6. AVOCADO DEVILED EGGS

Ingredients:

- 6 hard-boiled eggs, peeled and halved
- 1 ripe avocado, mashed
- 1 tbsp lime juice
- 1 tbsp fresh cilantro, chopped
- Salt and pepper to taste

Prep Time: 10 minutes
Cooking Time: N/A
Servings: 6

Instructions:

1. Remove yolks from hard-boiled eggs and place in a bowl.
2. Add mashed avocado, lime juice, cilantro, salt, and pepper.
3. Mix until smooth.
4. Spoon the avocado mixture into the egg whites.
5. Serve immediately.

CHAPTER 10

DESSERTS

ENJOYING DESSERTS RESPONSIBLY

Managing diabetes doesn't mean you have to give up desserts entirely. With thoughtful ingredient choices and portion control, you can still enjoy sweet treats without compromising your blood sugar levels. Here are some tips for enjoying desserts responsibly:

- **Choose Low-Sugar Options:** Opt for desserts made with natural sweeteners or reduced sugar.
- **Incorporate Fiber and Protein:** Including fiber and protein in your desserts can help slow the absorption of sugar and prevent blood sugar spikes.
- **Practice Portion Control:** Enjoy desserts in small portions to satisfy your sweet tooth without overindulging.

RECIPES

1. CHOCOLATE CHIA PUDDING

Ingredients:

- 1/4 cup chia seeds
- 1 cup unsweetened almond milk
- 2 tbsp unsweetened cocoa powder
- 1 tbsp maple syrup or sweetener of choice
- 1 tsp vanilla extract

Prep Time: 5 minutes
Cooking Time: 2 hours (chilling time)
Servings: 2

Instructions:

1. In a bowl, whisk together almond milk, cocoa powder, maple syrup, and vanilla extract.
2. Stir in chia seeds.
3. Cover and refrigerate for at least 2 hours or until the mixture thickens.
4. Stir well before serving.

2. BAKED APPLES WITH CINNAMON

Ingredients:

- 4 apples, cored

- 1/4 cup chopped walnuts
- 2 tbsp raisins
- 1 tsp ground cinnamon
- 1 tbsp maple syrup or honey

Prep Time: 10 minutes
Cooking Time: 30 minutes
Servings: 4

Instructions:

1. Preheat oven to 350°F (175°C).
2. Place apples in a baking dish.
3. In a bowl, combine chopped walnuts, raisins, cinnamon, and maple syrup.
4. Stuff the mixture into the apples.
5. Bake for 30 minutes or until apples are tender.
6. Serve warm.

3. ALMOND FLOUR COOKIES

Ingredients:

- 2 cups almond flour
- 1/4 cup coconut oil, melted
- 1/4 cup maple syrup or sweetener of choice
- 1 tsp vanilla extract
- 1/2 tsp baking soda
- Pinch of salt

Prep Time: 10 minutes
Cooking Time: 12 minutes
Servings: 12 cookies

Instructions:

1. Preheat oven to 350°F (175°C).
2. In a bowl, combine almond flour, melted coconut oil, maple syrup, vanilla extract, baking soda, and salt.
3. Mix until a dough forms.
4. Roll dough into balls and place on a baking sheet.
5. Flatten each ball slightly with a fork.
6. Bake for 12 minutes or until golden brown.
7. Let cool on a wire rack before serving.

4. BERRY SORBET

Ingredients:

- 2 cups mixed berries (strawberries, blueberries, raspberries)
- 1/4 cup water
- 2 tbsp lemon juice
- 1 tbsp honey or sweetener of choice

Prep Time: 5 minutes
Cooking Time: 2 hours (freezing time)
Servings: 4

Instructions:

1. In a blender, combine mixed berries, water, lemon juice, and honey.
2. Blend until smooth.
3. Pour mixture into a shallow dish and freeze for at least 2 hours.
4. Scrape with a fork to create a sorbet texture before serving.

5. PEANUT BUTTER ENERGY BALLS

Ingredients:

- 1 cup rolled oats
- 1/2 cup natural peanut butter
- 1/4 cup honey
- 1/4 cup flaxseeds
- 1/4 cup dark chocolate chips

Prep Time: 10 minutes
Cooking Time: N/A
Servings: 12 balls

Instructions:

1. In a bowl, combine rolled oats, peanut butter, honey, flaxseeds, and dark chocolate chips.
2. Mix until well combined.
3. Roll mixture into 1-inch balls.
4. Store in the refrigerator until ready to eat.

6. LEMON YOGURT PARFAIT

Ingredients:

- 1 cup plain Greek yogurt
- 1 tbsp lemon juice
- 1 tbsp honey
- 1/2 cup granola
- 1/2 cup fresh berries

Prep Time: 5 minutes
Cooking Time: N/A
Servings: 2

Instructions:

1. In a bowl, mix Greek yogurt, lemon juice, and honey.
2. In serving glasses, layer yogurt mixture, granola, and fresh berries.
3. Repeat layers and serve immediately.

CONCLUSION

Congratulations on taking the first step towards a healthier lifestyle with the "Supreme Diabetic Cookbook for Beginners." This journey is about more than just managing your diabetes; it's about embracing a balanced, nutritious diet that enhances your overall well-being.

EMBRACING A HEALTHY LIFESTYLE

As you've discovered throughout this cookbook, managing diabetes doesn't mean giving up delicious food. By making informed choices, you can enjoy a variety of tasty meals while maintaining stable blood sugar levels. Here are some key takeaways:

- **Balance and Variety:** Incorporate a mix of lean proteins, healthy fats, and high-fiber carbohydrates into your meals. This balance helps stabilize blood sugar and provides essential nutrients.
- **Mindful Eating:** Pay attention to portion sizes and savor each bite. Mindful eating can help you enjoy your meals more and recognize when you're full.
- **Regular Monitoring:** Keep track of your blood sugar levels, especially when trying new recipes

or ingredients. Understanding how different foods affect your body is crucial for effective diabetes management.

STAYING MOTIVATED

Maintaining a healthy diet can be challenging, but staying motivated is key. Here are some tips to keep you on track:

- **Set Realistic Goals:** Set achievable goals for your dietary habits and celebrate your progress, no matter how small.
- **Find Support:** Connect with friends, family, or a support group to share your journey. Having a support system can provide encouragement and accountability.
- **Keep Learning:** Stay informed about diabetes management and nutrition. The more you know, the better equipped you'll be to make healthy choices.

Thank you for choosing the "Supreme Diabetic Cookbook for Beginners." May it inspire you to cook delicious meals, embrace a healthier lifestyle, and enjoy the benefits of balanced nutrition.

Made in the USA
Monee, IL
29 July 2024